Fay and the Jay

by Liza Charlesworth • illustrated by Jim Paillot

SCHOLASTIC INC.

New York • Toronto • London • Auckland • Sydney
Mexico City • New Delhi • Hong Kong • Buenos Aires

Designed by Grafica, Inc.
ISBN: 978-0-545-68622-8
Copyright © 2009 by Lefty's Editorial Services.
All rights reserved. Published by Scholastic Inc.
SCHOLASTIC, LET'S LEARN READERS™, and associated logos are trademarks
and/or registered trademarks of Scholastic Inc.

12 11 10 9 8 7 6 5 4 3 2 1   14 15 16 17 18 19/0

Printed in China.

What Is a Word Family?
A word family is a group of words that rhyme and share the same spelling pattern, such as *Fay*, *day*, and *jay*. Read this story to learn more *-ay* words!

This is **Fay**.
Fay is a member of the **Ay** family.

One **day** in **May**, a bird flew to **Fay**.
It was a blue and **gray jay**!

"Can you **stay**?" said **Fay**.
"We can **play** with my dog, **Ray**."

"**Okay**!" said the **jay**.
Then they **play**ed all **day**!

The next **day**, **Fay** said, "Can you **stay**?
We can **play** by the **bay**."

"**Okay**!" said the **jay**.
Then they **play**ed all **day**!

The next **day**, **Fay** said, "Can you **stay**?
We can **play** with my **clay**."

"**Okay**!" said the **jay**.
Then they **play**ed all **day**!

The next **day**, Fay said, "Can you **stay**?
We can **play** in the **spray**."

"**Okay**!" said the **jay**.
Then they **play**ed all **day**!

The next **day**, **Fay** said, "Can you **stay**?
We can build a nest from **hay**."

"**Okay**!" said the **jay**.
"Now I can **stay** forever."
Yay!

Word Family House

Point to the -*ay* word in each room and read it aloud.

ray	say	way
jay	hay	day
may	Fay	bay
clay		stay
play		tray

Word Family Rhymes

Point to the rhyming pair that completes each sentence.

> **WORD BOX**
>
> bay stay   ray play
>
> gray day
>
> stray jay   hay pay

1 A lost bird is a _____ _____.

2 A rainy morning is a _____ _____.

3 A vacation at the ocean is a _____ _____.

4 Having fun in the sun is _____ _____.

5 Straw money is _____ _____.

Word Family Hunt

This tree contains eight -ay words. Can you find them all? Cover them with pennies or buttons.